HACKERS: BEHIND THE CODE

12 INCREDIBLE FACTS ABOUT CYBER-CRIMINALS

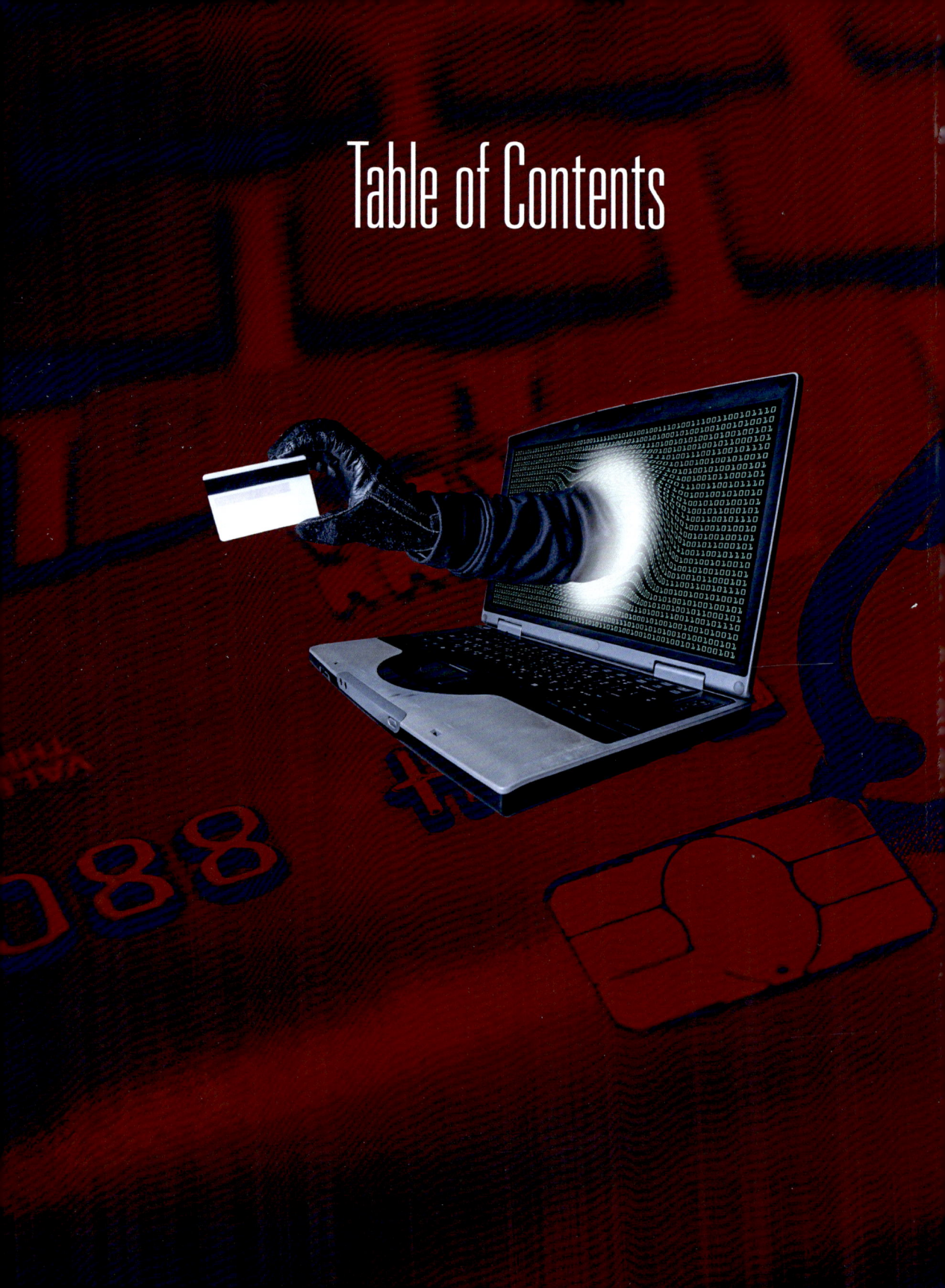
Table of Contents

1. Cybercriminals Are Digital Thieves	5
2. Internet Robbers Can Hide Anywhere	8
3. Cybercriminals Use Secret Codes	11
4. The Dark Web Is a Secret Internet	14
5. Cybercriminals Pretend to Be Someone Else	17
6. Digital Forensic Analysts Look for Clues	21
7. Some Hackers Begin as Teenagers	24
8. Cybersecurity Stops Bad Hackers	27
9. Some Hackers Work Together	30
10. Some Criminals Target Video Games	34
11. Most Cybercriminals Do Not Make Much Money	37
12. Cybercrime Can Target Anyone	40
Fact Sheet	44
Glossary	46
For More Information	47
Index	48

Be careful what information you type into websites.

Cybercriminals Are *Digital Thieves*

How much time are you online every day? Probably more than you think. Especially if you have devices using the internet. Lightbulbs and doorbells may be connected online. These connections make our lives easier. But they also create a new opportunity for crime.

Cybercriminals are thieves. They use computers or the internet to commit crimes. They can hack into any device. These hackers might work alone or on a team. They hide their **identities** online. It makes them harder to catch.

The goal of most cybercriminals is to make money. They steal information online. They run **scams**. The scams target everyone from single people to large companies. They trick people into revealing sensitive information. This includes social security numbers and credit card details. Then they can commit **fraud**. Some cybercriminals send out **malware**. This attacks devices. The hackers may spy on governments. They can lock systems and then demand a **ransom**. The list can go on. There are many ways these digital thieves can cause harm.

Cybercriminals can be tricky to catch. The internet is a vast space. It can be easy for them to hide their trail. Plus, hackers are always changing their ways. As technology advances, so do their methods and tools.

2,244 Number of attacks daily on four computers used in a US-based study.

That's an attack every 39 seconds. • Using a strong password helps guard against these attacks. • Avoid using common passwords like "123456" and "password."

Credit card information is often targeted by hackers.

Internet Robbers Can Hide *Anywhere*

2

One of the greatest benefits of the internet is connectivity. Someone in California can wish a friend in Finland happy birthday instantly. That's almost 5,600 miles (9,012 kilometers) apart! But not everyone uses the internet for good. Criminals can commit crimes from far away too. They don't need to be in the same country as their target. All they need is an internet connection.

Far away targets help thieves hide who they are. It's difficult to track crime across country borders. These criminals also use **cryptocurrency**. This is a type of online money. It allows hackers to be **anonymous**. People use a private key to move funds. Trades are recorded on public blockchains. Anyone can see them. They can follow the sale. But criminals move the money quickly. Tracing it overseas is almost impossible. Different countries have different rules on crypto. And

Think About It
Why would someone prefer using crypto instead of regular money?

not all countries work well with others. Criminals use crypto for payment. They also use it for scams.

Agencies like the FBI and CIA track down cybercriminals. They use digital forensics. These professionals analyze online data. They find clues that can lead to the criminals' doorstep.

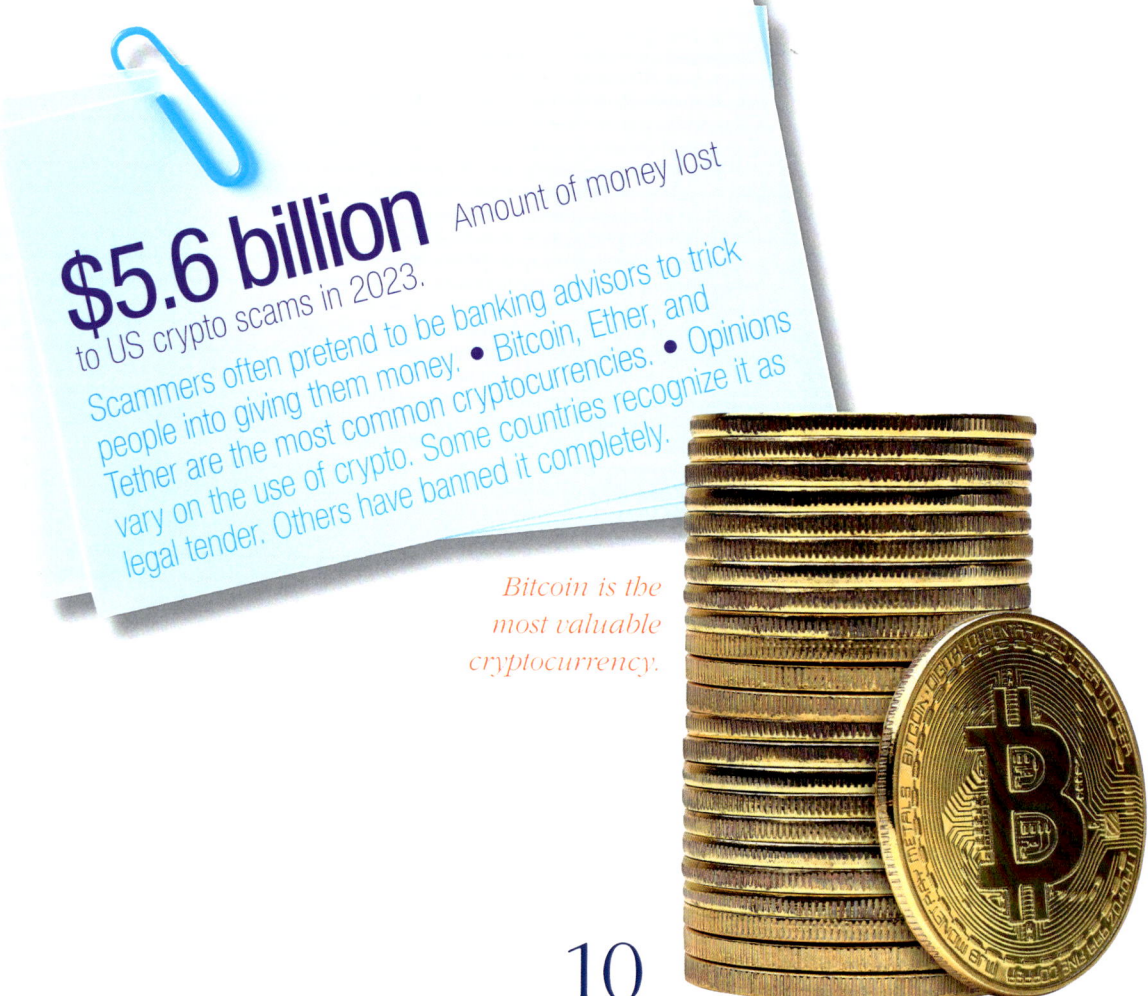

$5.6 billion Amount of money lost to US crypto scams in 2023. Scammers often pretend to be banking advisors to trick people into giving them money. • Bitcoin, Ether, and Tether are the most common cryptocurrencies. • Opinions vary on the use of crypto. Some countries recognize it as legal tender. Others have banned it completely.

Bitcoin is the most valuable cryptocurrency.

Cybercriminals Use *Secret Codes*

3

We use passwords every day. They unlock devices. You might use a code to unlock your front door. Codes give us access to private spaces. This applies to computers too. Online spaces can store personal information. They may keep other kinds of data safe.

Cybercriminals want access to these places. They might want to steal data. They may want to control the device remotely. They have a few methods for these cyberattacks.

Secret codes give them access to devices. Any program or code that hurts devices is called malware. Trojan horses sneak past people. These programs look normal. But they have code that takes over a machine. Backdoors create a secret way into devices.

The most common malware is a computer **virus**. It is also the most harmful. Like a cold, a computer can pass on the virus. Each computer becomes a "zombie." They are used by hackers to do bad things. The hackers can steal data on a larger scale. The zombie computers hide their identities.

People can download programs that find and warn about malware attacks.

MAFIABOY

In 2000, a 16-year-old boy knocked out CNN, Yahoo, Amazon, and eBay. He was known online as Mafiaboy. He used a zombie network. There were millions of computers. It was one of the largest Distributed Denial of Service (DDoS) attacks ever. These attacks overwhelm a system. They slow down websites and may cause the sites to crash.

80 Percent of spam messages sent by zombie machines.

There are millions of zombie computers in the world. • A quarter of these computers are in the United States alone. • Computers may have to be erased and rebuilt to get rid of the virus.

The Dark Web Is a *Secret Internet*

4

Digital thieves use different methods to get what they want. Some steal money directly. They trick people into sharing bank accounts or sending them money. Others steal data and information. Then they demand the company to pay a ransom to get it back. They can also sell the information. Bank accounts. Passwords. Social security numbers. Any personal data has a price tag. You just need to know where to sell it.

You probably haven't seen those things for sale. That's because it's illegal to sell them. Amazon, eBay, and other retailers obey laws about what people can sell on their sites. Plus, these sites are open to everyone. It would be easy to find the person selling an item. The police could quickly catch a hacker this way.

Cybercriminals sell this data on the **dark web**. Getting to this online space requires a special web browser.

PROTECTING FREE SPEECH

Sometimes people know damaging information. They want to share it without getting into trouble. The dark web hosts platforms like SecureDrop. SecureDrop gives people a place to share privately. Activists can use these platforms. So can people who live in harsh nations. They can communicate and stay safe. Their views can be heard.

The dark web can be a place to find many types of malware, like ransomware.

This browser has unique security settings. It can visit web addresses that end in a unique domain, like .radish instead of .com. It is where people buy stolen goods. There are also illegal items and services available. There are even kits to run scams.

The dark web isn't only for criminals. News outlets and government agencies use it too. They can pass along information in secret. Spies do too. Their identity stays safe. No one knows who they are.

$400 Opening bid in a dark web auction for 600 YouTube logins. The winning bidder can use the logins to take over the accounts. • Many YouTubers rely on the money they make off their channels. They are willing to pay to get their accounts back. • Logins are often stolen from computers infected with malware.

Cybercriminals Pretend to Be *Someone Else*

Hackers are the ultimate **impersonators**. Online criminals often pretend to be trustworthy. They ask nicely for money or favors. They often pretend to be a company or person you know. They may ask for a login or credit card. This is known as **phishing**. It is the most common form of cybercrime.

Experts guess that over 3 billion phishing messages are sent every day worldwide. Email providers try to block these messages. They are flagged as spam. They go to a different folder. But some messages still make it through.

Phishing through texts and apps is becoming more common. This is called smishing. One reason for this is two-factor authentication (2FA). 2FA is a security feature. It sends text messages with a code to access an app. Smishing fakes these texts. They ask users to respond with their password or other private information. Research shows that people trust text messages more than emails. People have their guard down over text messages.

It is possible to protect yourself. The key is to think carefully. Does the message sound strange? Is it unlike the person they claim to be? Call or message that person in another way. Is the message forceful or pushing you to act quickly? That's another sign. Phishers don't want you to have time to think. You are more likely to catch their tricks.

Phishers send out many messages hoping to catch a few unknowing victims.

1 in 5 Number of phishing emails that come from Russia.

- Attacks from Russian sources are especially tricky.
- Russian phishers are very good at faking real messages.
- Emails are still the most popular phishing practice.

Think About It

Imagine you receive a message from a teacher. They want your password to an app. How would you decide if it was real or not?

Digital Forensic Analysts *Look for Clues*

Imagine finding a huge mess in your kitchen. There are crumbs everywhere! You want to find who did this. What clues would you look for? Is there a trail of crumbs? Digital forensics works the same way. It is a branch of computer science. Experts look for clues left behind by criminals. They comb through data. Small digital crumbs can help solve cybercrime cases.

An analyst looks through different types of data. They look at a suspect's internet history. They can guess someone's location based on phone records. Every online device has an IP address. This includes a location too. Analysts can also follow the money trail. It may lead back to the criminal.

Every click online leaves a trail. This is called a digital footprint. Every message sent. Every post or photo liked. Every comment left. All of this is recorded and

saved in a footprint. Messages in chats can tell a lot. They can show locations, the type of devices used, and more. The type of device and system can be useful too. They provide a look into the suspect's file system. An analyst may be able to restore deleted data. The system can give hints about online activities. It might have access to the dark web.

More and more countries are helping with digital forensics. The analysts work together. Then it's easier to track cybercriminals across borders.

Phone data can be very helpful in catching criminals.

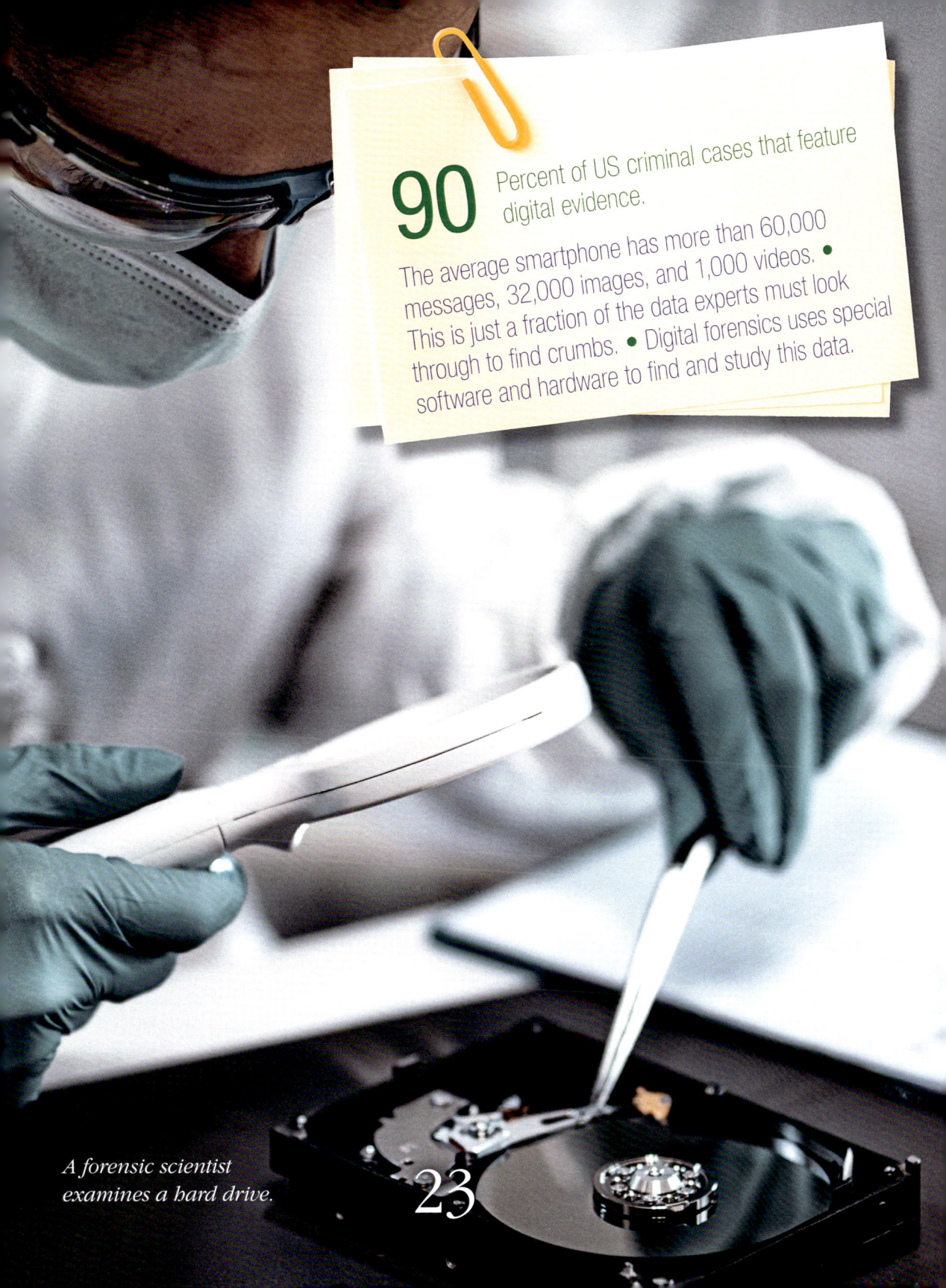

90 Percent of US criminal cases that feature digital evidence.

The average smartphone has more than 60,000 messages, 32,000 images, and 1,000 videos. • This is just a fraction of the data experts must look through to find crumbs. • Digital forensics uses special software and hardware to find and study this data.

A forensic scientist examines a hard drive.

Some Hackers Begin as *Teenagers*

7

Have you ever found something online that didn't work right? Maybe a button was mislabeled. Or an action didn't match what you expected. These errors on websites are called "bugs." Bugs can cause major issues. They may reveal private information by mistake. Kids are often introduced to hacking through "bug hunting." They face a choice. Act responsibly and report the bug? Or use it for their own gain?

Jack Cable was 15 years old when he found a bug. It was a big one. Someone could have used it to steal money. Instead, Cable reported it to the company. This introduced him to "bug bounties." These programs are run by companies. They reward people who find bugs. Cable went on to compete in more programs. He even won first place in "Hack the Air Force." It was a challenge run by the US Department of Defense. This

19 Average age of cybercriminals caught in the United States.

The average age of anyone arrested for a US crime is 37. • Sometimes, cybercriminals forget to hide information about themselves. This can lead the police to their computer. • The government has hired hackers for cybersecurity.

LEARNING TO DEBUG Bug hunting teaches patience and persistence. It takes time to find errors in code. And it takes much longer to come across impactful bugs. Over time, hackers get better at finding bugs. These are also known as **vulnerabilities**. And as hackers improve, their coding skills grow as well.

led to him working for the Pentagon. Cable was on *Time Magazine's* list of "25 Most Influential Teens of 2018." Today, he is a respected computer security researcher. All this from making the right choice in reporting a bug.

Bug hunting is just one introduction to hacking. But it's often a hacker's first taste of working outside a system. Small bugs can become bigger hacks. As kids grow their skills, they face an important choice. Use their skills to make the internet safer? Or choose cybercrime?

Computer bugs are named after a real bug once found in a machine.

Cybersecurity Stops *Bad Hackers*

8

Thinking about cybercrime can be overwhelming. There are many ways digital thieves can steal from people. But for every crime they can commit, there's a way to stop them.

Cybersecurity protects people online. It can be a type of job or a set of rules. Or it can be an app that keeps devices safe. Experts in this field create layers of defense. These layers help stop criminals. A criminal might break through one layer. But it is harder to get past two or three layers.

Many cybersecurity pros have college degrees in fields outside of computer science. That's because stopping hackers takes more than knowing how to code. Good communication and problem-solving skills are just as important. Pros need to think like a hacker. And in some cases, they used to be hackers!

While helpful, a college degree isn't always needed for a job in cybersecurity.

Cybersecurity both stops and responds to attacks. One might think they could never be hacked. But that's not realistic. Not every security **breach** is a disaster. But not knowing how to handle a breach? That's a problem. Experts learn from attacks. They need to know how to stop and respond quickly.

TO BE BRIEF Think like the experts. Treat your passwords like your underwear! It's important to change both things regularly. Never share your passwords with other people. And finally? Keep them out of sight from other people. That goes for underwear too!

$10.5 trillion Worldwide estimated cost of cybercrime in 2025.

Cybercrime is becoming more profitable than the illegal drug trade. • This amount includes more than just stolen money. • It includes restoring data and lost work time, plus the cost of the investigation.

Cybersecurity picks up the pieces after an attack and makes the system stronger.

Some Hackers Work Together

9

The best teams **leverage** skillsets. On a baseball team, pitchers rarely hit home runs. They focus their strength on pitching. Their ability to throw a fastball helps the team more than their batting. Other players are strong hitters. They spend more time in batting practice. To win, the team needs a good balance of both types of players. Cybercriminals also come together. They create crime teams. And their goal is to take down big targets.

Hackers band together to combine their skills. A single hacker might be good at one kind of attack. Another might be able to code through security measures. A good cybersecurity plan has layers to it. Larger companies make tempting targets. They can pay larger ransoms. But they also have better security. A supervillain cyber team forms. Together, they have the skills to break through those layers.

These hacking squads are responsible for some of the biggest hacks in history. And they aren't always focused on making money. A group of Russian hackers calls themselves Fancy Bear. They've been sneaking into computers since 2008. They're known for spying on important people. In 2016, they were blamed for messing with the US presidential election. Cozy Bear, another Russian hacker squad, attacked the SolarWinds supply chain in 2020.

Hacker squads can be sneaky, scary, or sometimes cool. Sometimes they fight for justice. Others just want power or money. No matter what their goal is, they show us how powerful computers and the internet can be.

Hackers from different countries can easily work together online.

Think About It
Can you think of other examples of people combining their strengths? How did it make them stronger together than alone?

200,000 Number of computers the Lazarus Group infected with ransomware in 2014.

Lazarus Group is part of a cyber warfare group in North Korea. • In 2014, the group hacked Sony Pictures after the release of the movie The Interview. • The attack caused $4 billion in damage.

Some Criminals Target *Video Games*

10

There's a good rule to remember about hacking. If a device uses the internet, it can be hacked. This includes phone apps. In fact, the fastest growing area for digital criminals is mobile games. The global gaming industry made almost $200 billion in 2022. And criminals want a piece of it.

Some hackers target games specifically. It's easy for hackers to add malware to games. Keyloggers can record screens and track when users are typing. It's an easy way to learn someone's password. A person might use their device for banking. Or they use a password to protect their private information. A hacker can gain all that data.

Even if you don't download games often, hackers can wreak havoc. Stealing Fortnite and Roblox accounts is becoming more common. Hackers often use phishing

1.6 Terabytes of data stolen by ransomware group Rhysida.

The group stole data from Insomniac Games in 2023. • The company refused to pay the $2 million ransom. • The data was shared online. • The breach revealed games that were under development to other gaming companies.

Young gamers can be an easy target for online data.

35

scams. They offer to help someone level up in the game. Then they ask for login or other data. Or they might create a **spoof** website. You log in thinking it's real, but now the hacker has your data. Cybercriminals are tricky! Once they know your login, they have your account. What if you use the same username and password for other accounts? Now they can log in everywhere!

You can keep your game accounts safe. Never share your login information. Be wary of cheat codes found online. Use 2FA whenever possible. Finally, keep an eye out for strange things happening on your account. If you see something, change your password!

Think About It
Do you play video games? When was the last time you looked at your account's security settings?

Most Cybercriminals Do Not Make *Much Money*

11

Many news companies talk about the financial impact of a hack. Headlines claim hacks cost millions or billions of dollars. It sounds like hackers made that much money. But that's not the case. Hackers get a relatively small piece.

When a company pays for a cyberattack, it's more than just the ransom. It includes the cost of fixing whatever the hackers broke. This is lost work time for the company. The company includes this cost. The cybersecurity may be enhanced after an attack. This price is included. The overall number is high because these costs are high.

There's also the fact that cybercrime is illegal. The rewards of hacking don't outweigh the risks. Especially when the risks include going to prison!

The best way to make money as a hacker is by stopping other hackers. **Ethical** hackers make their living by finding vulnerabilities. They hack into computers to test security, not to steal. They do this with the company's permission. They work within a certain set of rules. But they still think like a bad hacker. They need to know trends in the cybercriminal world. This helps them build strong defenses. It also makes the internet safer for everyone.

BOOM OR BUST? Verizon created a study in 2024. They looked at how much money criminals made from ransomware attacks. Sixty percent saw no profit. Some made $1. The average was about $100. Making money as a cybercriminal is like playing the lottery. Sometimes a criminal will hit it big. But most don't earn much at all.

Some bad hackers swap sides and become an ethical hacker.

$211,000 Average yearly pay of a US ethical hacker.

Tech companies pay ethical hackers the most. These include Google and IBM. • Many ethical hacker jobs don't list a college degree. But you do need certifications. • Research and teamwork are highly needed skills for ethical hacking.

Cybercrime Can Target *Anyone*

12

Imagine you're in a real-life treasure hunt. You finally reach the end of the hunt. A huge treasure chest sits in front of you. In the corner of your eye, you notice something doesn't look quite right. But you're focused on the treasure. As you reach out to touch the gold… BAM! A rope snaps around your hand! It was all a trap!

Cybercriminals act similarly. They create something that looks cool, or something that needs your immediate attention. But it's a trick to steal from as many people as possible. These criminals try to catch anyone in their tricks. This includes you, your parents, or an entire company. They even use images to get people to click on fake sites.

Remember that almost anything online could open you up to an attack. But practicing basic safety measures can protect you. It's like stopping criminals from coming into your home. Locking the door is one step. You wouldn't let a stranger in your home, right? And if someone tried, you would tell a trusted adult. A secure password is like a heavy door lock. Never share your private information, even with friends. But if you think you have been hacked, tell a parent or a teacher as soon as possible.

Getting hacked isn't anything to be ashamed of. The most important thing you can do is to tell someone. This is the first step to stop cyber criminals from hurting others!

Think About It
Think like a cybersecurity professional. If you were hacked, what's your plan?

42

80 Estimated percent of fake links for puppy sales.

These ads target internet users in their late teens to early 20s. • The scammer lists the puppy for a low price, then demands money for shipping, shots, and other costs. • Yorkies and French Bulldogs are the most common breeds with scam listings.

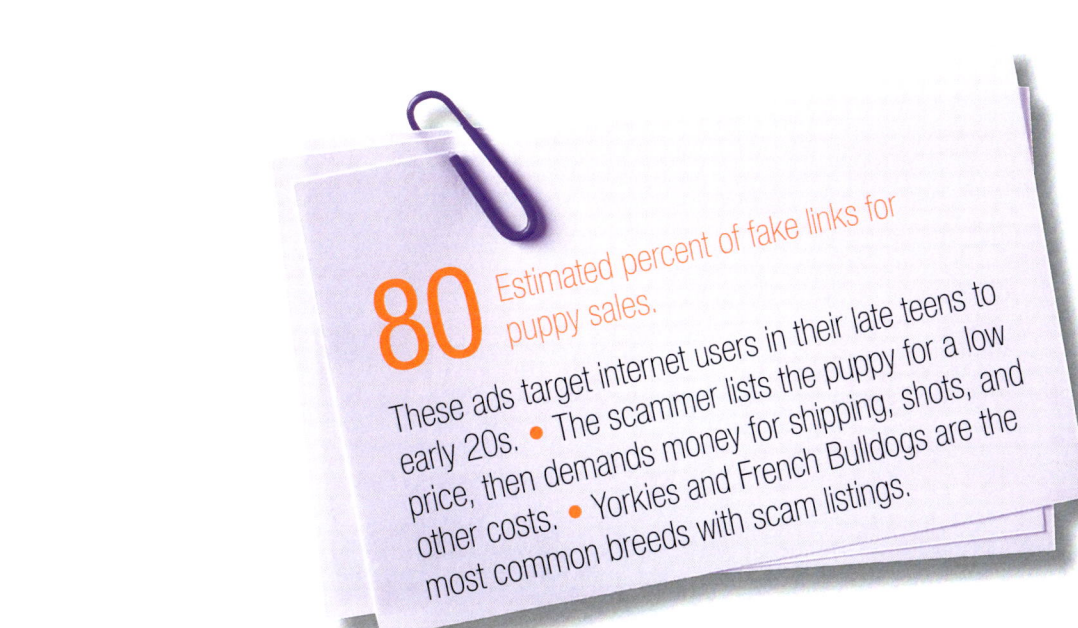

Scammers try to lure in people like a mouse trap.

Fact

- Not all criminals are outsiders. Some of the worst threats can come from a company's own employees. These "insiders" don't always have bad intent. Between 68 and 95 percent of hacks are due to internal error. But some insiders actively work against the company. They do it out of anger. Or someone is paying them for information.

- Some cybercriminal groups are backed by governments. They receive funding and protection. In return, they spy on other countries. They may cause disruptions. China, Russia, Iran, and North Korea are suspected of this. They may support over 70 percent of cyber spying.

Sheet

- Many hackers use artificial intelligence (AI) tools. Cybercriminals do too. This helps make their scams more believable. AI can clone voices. Scammers can pretend to be someone else. AI can even create fake face and fingerprint data. This helps digital thieves commit fraud.

- Look closely when something seems wrong online. Hackers often create fake websites. The URLs look similar but have small errors. It may say "amazo.com" instead of "amazon.com."

- Use long passwords with many numbers and symbols. It's harder to steal more complex passwords. If it's too hard to remember, use a password manager. This software securely stores and creates your passwords. It acts like a digital vault for logins.

Glossary

anonymous
Not named or identified.

breach
A gap in a barrier or defense where someone can attack.

cryptocurrency
A digital money that only exists online and is controlled by a network of computers.

dark web
A part of the World Wide Web that is hidden from public view and requires specific software to access.

ethical
Following accepted rules of behavior.

fraud
The crime of using dishonest methods to take something valuable from another person.

identity
Who someone is, including their real name, address, birthdate, and other personal information.

impersonator
A person who pretends to be someone else.

leverage
To use something valuable to gain a desired result.

malware
Software that is designed to mess up, damage, or gain unauthorized access to a computer system.

phishing
The unlawful practice of sending messages that look believable in order to trick targets into giving out personal information.

ransom
Money that is paid in order to free something that has been captured.

scam
A dishonest way to make money by lying to people.

spoof
A humorous copy of something, done in a silly or exaggerated way.

virus
A program designed to harm a computer that can be spread secretly from one computer to another.

vulnerability
A flaw or weakness in a system or process that can be used by an attacker.

For More Information

Books

Abdo, Kenny. *Cyber Heists*. Minneapolis: Abdo Zoom, 2025.

Eason, Sarah. *Hunting a Hacker: Using Science to Crack Cybercrime*. Shropshire, UK: Cheriton Children's Books, 2023.

Lew, Kristi. *Cybercrime and You*. Rosen Publishing: New York, 2020.

Websites

Cybercrimes and You
www.prageru.com/video/cybercrimes-and-you

Hackers and Cyber Attacks
tpt.pbslearningmedia.org/resource/hackers-cyber-attacks-crash-course-cs/

About the Author

Meghan Hatalla is a Minnesota-based writer and UX researcher exploring the intersection of people, technology, and storytelling. She critically examines everything from enterprise AI to historical disasters to create engaging nonfiction for curious minds. When not writing, she's exploring forests, lifting heavy things, or chasing down obscure facts.

Index

bug hunting, 24, 26

Cable, Jack, 24, 26
costs, 29, 33, 37
cryptocurrency, 8, 10
cybersecurity, 24, 27, 28, 30, 37

dark web, 14, 15, 16, 22
DDoS attacks, 13
digital footprints, 21–22
digital forensics, 10, 21–22, 23

ethical hackers, 38, 39

fraud, 6, 45

hacking groups, 30–31, 33, 35, 44

international borders, 8, 22

Mafiaboy, 13
malware, 6, 11–12, 16, 34

online safety, 11, 27, 28, 36, 38, 40–41, 45

passwords, 6, 11, 14, 18, 20, 28, 34, 36, 41, 45
personal information, 11, 14
phishing, 17–18, 19, 34

profit from crimes, 16, 37–38

ransoms, 6, 14, 30, 33, 35, 37, 38

scams, 5, 10, 16, 36, 43, 45
SecureDrop, 15
smishing, 17
spoof websites, 36

teen hackers, 13, 24, 26
two-factor authentication, 17, 36

video games, 34, 35, 36
viruses, 12, 13

TOP RANK is published by Black Rabbit Books, P.O. Box 227, Mankato, MN, 56002. • Copyright © 2026 Black Rabbit Books. All rights reserved. No part of this book may be reproduced in any form without written permission from the publisher. • Designed by Danny Nanos • Photographs © Shutterstock/Andrew E Gardner, 29, Andrey Burmakin, 27, Andrey_Popov, 44, A9 STUDIO, 15, 30, Belinda Pretorius, 48, carballo, 20, Chatham172, 42–43, CeltStudio, 32–33, David Gyung, 34, DD Images, 16, Eduardo Frederiksen, 36, Hakim Ullah ID 4268939, 45, HappyAngel 888, 38, Harun Ozmen, 10, Igor Kyrylytsya, cover, 1, IvaFoto, 13, janews, 12, Jirsak, 35, Jolygon, 46–47, kinziramtane, 7, KKulikov, 28, Leonidas Santana, 36, Lisa-S, 4–5, Maxx-Studio, 41, Mega Pixel, 27, Microgen, 23, Midnight Studio TH, 39, Miha Creative, 40, Mzynasx, 45, ParinPix, 17, Peyker, 24, Phubes Juwattana, 45, Poravute Siriphiroon, 22, PX Media, 31, Sergey Toronto, 26, Shawn Hempel, 21, SteafPong88, 8–9, StepanPopov, 14, Thichaa, 37, TimeStopper69, 2, 7, wk1003mike, 2–3, 11, 18–19, worker, 25, xpixel, 25, Yeti studio, 6 • Printed in the United States of America.
Library of Congress Cataloging-in-Publication Data: Names: Hatalla, Meghan author | Title: 12 incredible facts about cybercriminals / by Meghan Hatalla. | Other titles: Twelve incredible facts about cybercriminals | Description: Mankato, MN: Top Rank, an imprint of Black Rabbit Books, [2026] | Series: Hackers: behind the code | Includes bibliographical references and index. | Audience: Ages 9–13 | Audience: Grades 4–6 | Identifiers: LCCN 2025021462 (print) | LCCN 2025021463 (ebook) | ISBN 9781645825203 library binding | ISBN 9781645825388 paperback | ISBN 9781645825562 ebook | Subjects: LCSH: Computer crimes—Juvenile literature | Hackers—Juvenile literature | Criminals—Juvenile literature | Classification: LCC HV6773 .H386 2026 (print) | LCC HV6773 (ebook) | DDC 364.16/8—dc23/eng/20250701 | LC record available at https://lccn.loc.gov/2025021462 | LC ebook record available at https://lccn.loc.gov/2025021463

HACKERS: BEHIND THE CODE

12 INCREDIBLE FACTS ABOUT HACKTIVISTS

Black Rabbit Books

Table of Contents

#	Chapter	Page
1.	Hacking + Activism = Hacktivism	5
2.	Hacktivists Are Cyber Ninjas	8
3.	Hacktivism Can Help Stop Bad Guys	11
4.	Hacktivists Fight to Make Big Changes	14
5.	Eco-Hacktivists Support Environmental and Animal Rights	17
6.	Hacktivists Usually Don't Target People	21
7.	Cablegate Leaks Thousands of Classified Documents	24
8.	Some Famous Hacktivists Stay Hidden	27
9.	Hacktivists Hide to Protect Themselves and Their Cause	30
10.	Hacktivists Spy on Spies	34
11.	Governments Create Laws to Stop Hacktivists	37
12.	A Secret War Online	40
	Fact Sheet	44
	Glossary	46
	For More Information	47
	Index	48

Parks' actions paved the way for legal and social changes in the Civil Rights Movement.

Think About It
What causes are you passionate about? What would you fight for?

Hacking
+ Activism
= *Hacktivism*

Many people have demanded change over the years. They fought for it in different ways. Women, Black people, and others fought for the right to vote. They formed large protests. Change can begin on a smaller scale too. The action of one person can spark a change. The story of Rosa Parks is well-known. She was tired after a long day of work. She boarded a bus in Montgomery, Alabama, to ride home. A white man demanded she stand so he could sit on the bus. She refused to give up her seat. This was against the law at the time. Parks was in trouble for refusing to stand. Her action started a huge bus protest.

These are acts of **activism**. Activists come in many different forms. They might be acting alone. Or they might be in a crowd of thousands. The number of people can change. But it needs to begin with someone.

Hackers can be activists too. Using hacking in this way is called "hacktivism." It refers to people using computer hacking for political or social issues. Learning to hack is easier than ever. More activists are using hacking to draw attention to their causes. With devices all around us, this is makes getting the word out quick and easy.

1996 Year a hacker named Omega created the word "hacktivist."

Omega is a member of the hacking group Cult of the Dead Cow. • The number of hackers grew in the 1990s. • This is when personal computers became more common.

Martin Luther King, Jr., is another famous activist for civil rights.

Hacktivists Are *Cyber Ninjas*

2

Hacktivists work in a similar way to hackers. Some sneak into computer systems without being noticed. They might **deface** a website to protest an issue. They edit content and add messages for their cause. Other hacktivists create a Distributed Denial of Service (DDoS) attack. This uses **malware**. It floods a website with online traffic. The site gets overwhelmed. It crashes and users can't use it.

Another goal is finding data to support their cause. Let's say you support animal rights. You think a company is using cats for harmful experiments. As a hacktivist, you access their computer network. You look for any records mentioning cat experiments. This might be emails or reports. Then you can post these secrets. Sharing important secrets is called a "leak." Eventually, that leak can lead to something bigger.

20,000 Emails published by WikiLeaks in the 2016 Democratic National Committee hack. The leaked emails had private information, like social security numbers. • At least 12 Russian hackers were charged by the US Department of Justice. • The hackers believed they were acting in the best interests of Russia.

That is the goal of hacktivist leaks. They find information of different sizes. Then they release it.

The leaked information can get a company in trouble. This is one goal of hacktivists. If a company is doing something illegal, hacktivists want the world to know. The other goal is to draw attention. People might not realize cats are being used in experiments. Releasing data informs people. It sways public opinion. Others may become activists too.

HOME FOR LEAKS WikiLeaks is a website for leaks. Hacktivists can share secrets they find. They submit anonymously to avoid getting into trouble. The site posts secrets like hidden government or company files. Some say people deserve to know the truth of what's going on. Others think it can be dangerous or unfair.

Hacktivism Can Help Stop *Bad Guys*

3

Hackers can have a bad **reputation**. Some hackers cause problems and unrest. But others work to make the web safe. The difference between a good and bad hacker is their goal. Are they trying to harm? Or are they trying to stop or prevent harm?

Hacktivists are in this same space. They have double reputations. Some hacktivists do more harm than good. But some want to create a safer, fairer world. Some stop bad people from hurting others. Hacktivists for social causes look for those at fault. They might target a company or government. They may even focus on **terrorists**.

In 2015, the hacktivist group Anonymous "declared war" on ISIS. ISIS took credit for acts of terrorism across the world. Thousands had been killed or

injured by ISIS. After another attack in Paris, France, Anonymous went to work. Their goal was to **disrupt** the main tools ISIS used to talk and gain new members. Anonymous sabotaged ISIS websites. They took down social media accounts. They removed videos. Anonymous showed how it's possible to impact a worldwide terrorist group. No one was killed or hurt. But ISIS suffered in other ways.

Syrian fighters raise their hands after a victory over ISIS.

100,000 Estimated number of pro-ISIS Twitter accounts shut down by Anonymous.

ISIS used Twitter to find new members and share information. • Anonymous also broke over 100 ISIS websites. • Even though Anonymous fought ISIS, their actions are still illegal.

Think About It Is it possible that wars could be fought online? How would one decide what actions are and are not okay?

Hacktivists Fight to Make *Big Changes*

4

The internet is a powerful tool. Even without hacking, one person can do a lot. Information can be stored and shared with millions. Big ideas can find the right audience. They can find the right people to make them happen. Hacktivists play a part in bringing big ideas to life. Their goal is to create social change. A hacker's skills can broaden a message. It can be a lifeline to the world.

Internet **censorship** is common in in the Middle East. They have stricter governments. The government controls websites and the news. It decides what information people receive. Hacktivists know how to work around these limits. They can help bring major change to these places.

The Arab Spring was a series of protests. They happened in the Middle East in the early 2010s.

100,000 Percent increase of daily use of Twitter for Egyptian users in 2011.

Around 15 million people participated in Egyptian protests. • Over 18 days, users livestreamed the revolution. • Due to these protests, citizens overthrew the president who had ruled for 30 years.

Hacktivists played an important role. They used tools like **proxies** and **VPNs** to avoid internet censorship. They leaked documents that proved the government was dishonest. Social media was used to organize protests. It was like a megaphone to the world.

Hacktivists helped protesters stay connected. It was effective too. Within a few months, the leadership fell in Yemen, Egypt, Libya, and Tunisia. Unrest has continued in the Middle East to the present day.

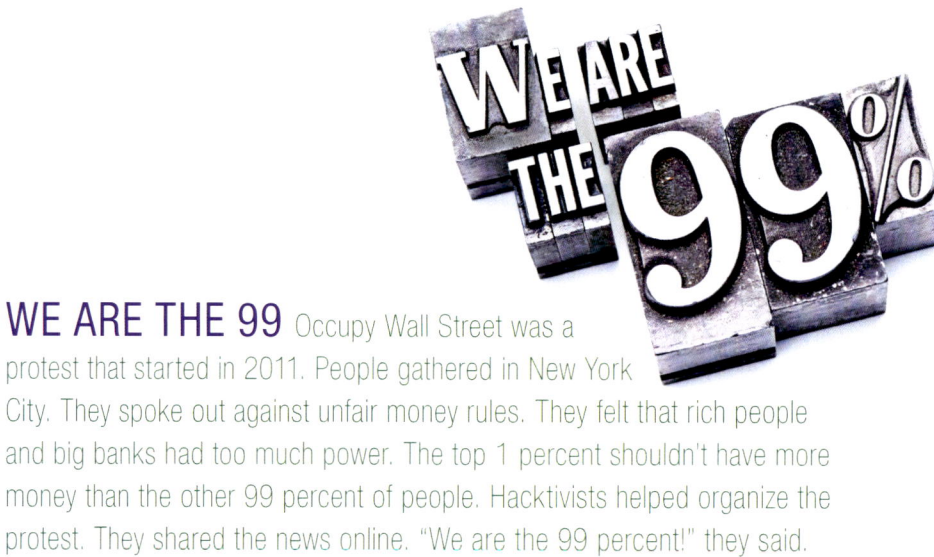

WE ARE THE 99 Occupy Wall Street was a protest that started in 2011. People gathered in New York City. They spoke out against unfair money rules. They felt that rich people and big banks had too much power. The top 1 percent shouldn't have more money than the other 99 percent of people. Hacktivists helped organize the protest. They shared the news online. "We are the 99 percent!" they said.

Eco-Hacktivists Support Environmental and Animal Rights

Eco-hacktivists fight against things that harm the planet. They mix hacking with environmental activism. They target companies responsible for pollution, deforestation, climate change, or animal cruelty. In a way, they speak up for those who don't have a voice.

A clear effect of eco-hacktivism is the changes at SeaWorld. SeaWorld is a chain of aquatic-themed parks. Until 2019, they were famous for their trained orcas. These whales are incredibly smart mammals. SeaWorld featured them in shows interacting with trainers. Some people do not agree with this practice.

Eco-hacktivists took to the internet on this issue. They created online operations called #OpSeaWorld, #OpWhales, and others. These operations directed eco-hacktivist attacks. They took down SeaWorld websites using DDoS attacks. They even snuck into a Twitter hashtag event run by SeaWorld. The event was called #AskSeaWorld. Hacktivists used the hashtag to explain the mistreatment of orcas.

SeaWorld got a lot of complaints. The company reacted to this. They phased out their orca breeding program. There are no more orcas in their shows. Eco-hacktivists weren't the only force for this change. But they helped. One measure of success for eco-hacktivism is companies changing their practices.

4.2 Terabytes of data leaked by eco-hacktivist group Guacamaya in 2022. That's like 1,000 full-length movies! • The data revealed pollution practices by a mining company in Guatemala. • It also showed proof of attempts to bribe the government and journalists in the country.

Two orcas perform during a SeaWorld show in 2009.

#OPERATIONWHAT?

#Op is short for operation. It is used by hacktivists to make threads of content online. It's easy to find the hashtag. Users can follow the news. This helps people connect to the bigger movement. It's a way to brand a digital movement!

Hacktivists Usually Don't *Target People*

Picking targets is different for hacktivists. A regular hacker will look for the quickest route to their goal. They like easy targets. The attack is usually not personal. Hacktivists are more selective. The attack is very personal. They look for connections to their cause. However, hacktivists rarely target specific people.

Some hacktivists aim to hold powerful systems accountable. They know that organizations, companies, and industries cause the most harm. Hacktivists want to rebalance power from those causing harm back to the public. They use their digital tools like a giant flashlight. They want to shine a light on big problems in hidden spaces.

One way that hacktivists do this is by modifying the public websites of their targets. A hacktivist breaks into a private website. Then they edit the site in some way. This raises awareness of both the hacker and their cause. DDoS strikes are another way to attack a website. The attacks cause a company website to become unusable. The downtime for a company can be terrible. It affects their public reputation and whether their business can function. Which, for a hacktivist, is exactly the point.

27,944 Printers hijacked by hacktivists in 2022 to show security issues.

Printer security is often overlooked. • The hacktivists wanted people to secure their printers before a bad hacker got to them. • They hacked the printers and printed out a guide on how to secure it.

Hacktivists Usually Don't *Target People*

Picking targets is different for hacktivists. A regular hacker will look for the quickest route to their goal. They like easy targets. The attack is usually not personal. Hacktivists are more selective. The attack is very personal. They look for connections to their cause. However, hacktivists rarely target specific people.

Some hacktivists aim to hold powerful systems accountable. They know that organizations, companies, and industries cause the most harm. Hacktivists want to rebalance power from those causing harm back to the public. They use their digital tools like a giant flashlight. They want to shine a light on big problems in hidden spaces.

One way that hacktivists do this is by modifying the public websites of their targets. A hacktivist breaks into a private website. Then they edit the site in some way. This raises awareness of both the hacker and their cause. DDoS strikes are another way to attack a website. The attacks cause a company website to become unusable. The downtime for a company can be terrible. It affects their public reputation and whether their business can function. Which, for a hacktivist, is exactly the point.

27,944 Printers hijacked by hacktivists in 2022 to show security issues.

Printer security is often overlooked. • The hacktivists wanted people to secure their printers before a bad hacker got to them. • They hacked the printers and printed out a guide on how to secure it.

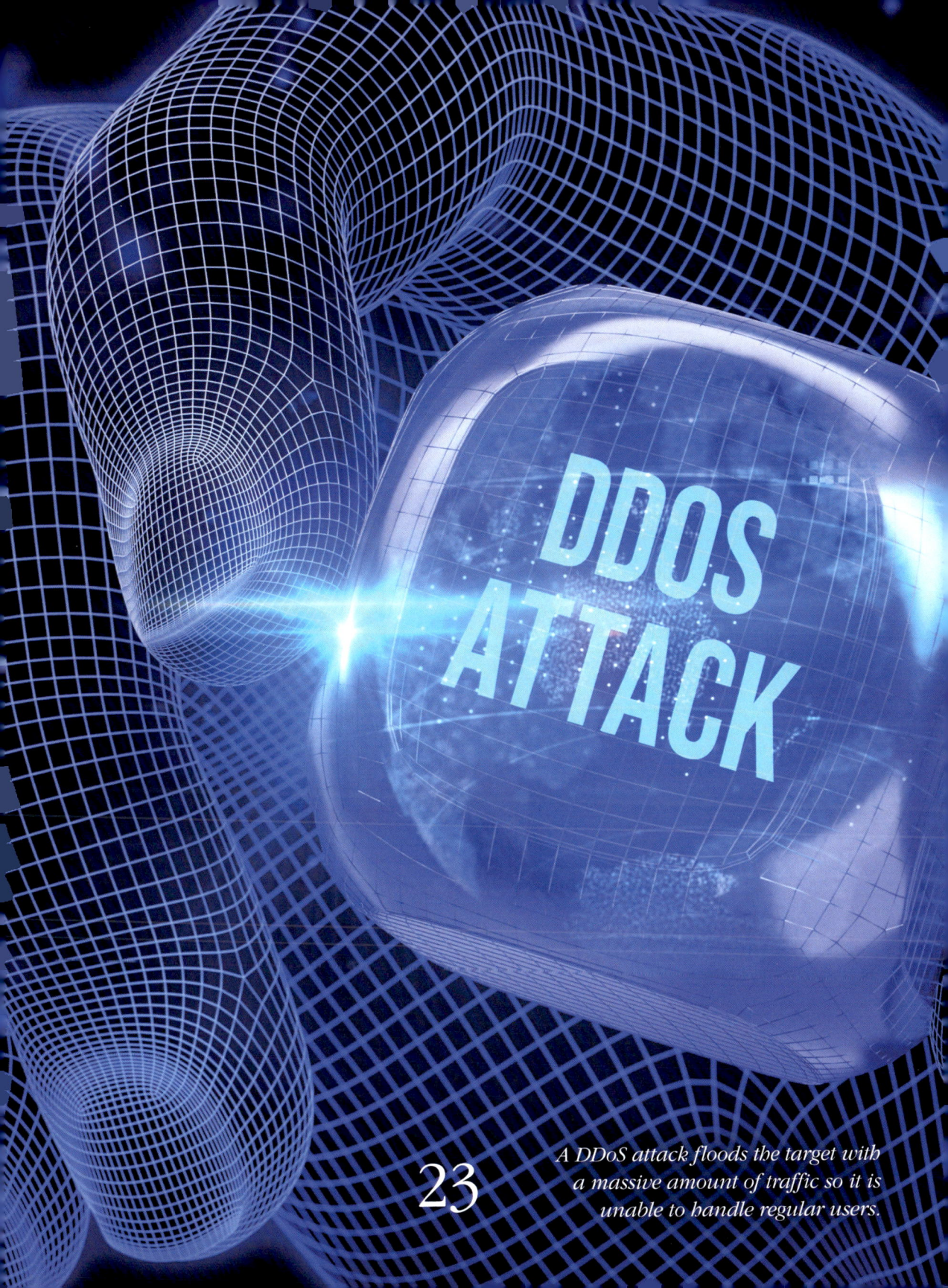

A DDoS attack floods the target with a massive amount of traffic so it is unable to handle regular users.

Cablegate Leaks Thousands of *Classified Documents*

Imagine that the teachers at your school shared a secret notebook. In it, they wrote their feelings about others. They wrote about difficult students. They wrote notes about other teachers and even the principal. Now imagine a student found that notebook. They make copies and share it with everyone. Yikes! What would the reaction be around the school? Some people might be embarrassed. Others would feel hurt. Some secrets might not be appropriate to share. They might make people angry. That's kind of what happened with Cablegate.

In 2010, Chelsea Manning leaked over 250,000 **cables**. It was the biggest US leak of **classified** records. Manning was an Army intelligence analyst at the time. She had access to national security data. Some messages were about the wars in Iraq and Afghanistan.

Think About It
Should the government be allowed to act in secret? Or do citizens have a right to always know what it does?

Some included bad things the military had done. Manning thought the public should know the truth. She wanted to hold governments accountable.

The cables were posted on WikiLeaks. The leak affected governments around the world. To some people, Manning was a hero. Others called her a traitor. Her actions were illegal.

Cablegate led to changes. Governments now handle secret information differently. The case also led to harsher punishments for leaks. Manning was sent to prison for 35 years. President Barack Obama shortened her sentence in 2017. She served seven years.

10 million Number of documents Wikileaks has published since 2006. • Wikileaks is a hacktivist space. • The site disrupts powerful organizations by releasing information. • It has published the most classified and sensitive data in history.

Some Famous Hacktivists *Stay Hidden*

8

Is it possible to be famous without anyone knowing who you are? Hacktivists balance this tightrope. They are known for their hacks. Some help overthrow governments. Some fight for human and animal rights. Others hack for environmental issues. And still, they are hidden. No one knows their identity.

Why do hacktivists hide? The most important reason is to avoid getting caught. If found, they could be arrested, fined, or jailed. Hacktivists often work in secret systems. Access to these systems isn't always legal. Hiding also keeps the focus on the message. A hacker's identity is less important than their goals.

Anonymous is one of the most famous hacktivist groups. Very few people know who they are. There isn't a single leader in the group. Members all wear the same mask. It is called a Guy Fawkes mask. It hides

The Guy Fawkes mask is famous from the film V for Vendetta.

their face while showing that they are part of one group. Anonymous acts when people are being treated unfairly.

Opinions vary on hacktivists. Some people think they go to the extreme to achieve their goal. But others see them as a modern Robin Hood. Or they are like a masked superhero. Hacktivists fight powerful people. They try to end **injustice**. And they are good at hacking in secret.

MOST EXTREME

Suicide hackers are people who do big, risky hacks. These hackers know that they will likely get caught. They break into powerful systems to share secrets. They protest unfair things. They do it for a cause, not for money. They take huge risks to stand up for what they believe in.

A statue of Robin Hood stands outside the Nottingham Castle in central England.

6,600 Number of pro-Russian hacktivist attacks between March 2022–24. The hacktivists spread pro-Russian messages. They blamed Ukraine for the Russian-Ukraine war. About 96 percent of the attacks targeted European countries. They tried to lessen the trust Europeans had with one another.

Hacktivists Hide to Protect Themselves *and Their Cause*

9

Imagine there is a new group at school. They start making new unfair rules. People get angry. Your friends want to push back. But they don't want to get in trouble. Hacktivists are like this. They use computers to push back. They work in secret. Getting caught could get them in big trouble. They use different tricks to stay hidden. These tricks are called OpSec, or operational security.

OpSec is a military word. But it can refer to anyone who wants to hide their tracks. It's a set of tips. It helps keep identities and data securely hidden. There is more than one way to do OpSec. Like a **cybersecurity** plan, hackers can create layers.

There are some common OpSec trends for hackers. Hacktivists often use fake names. They use tools with

encryption to share information. These tools are very difficult to crack. Hacktivists also hide their location. This includes their IP address. This makes it hard to track them. Even devices and operating systems can be hidden.

Hacktivists need to be careful. If they want to keep working for their cause, it's important not to get caught. These cyberactivists believe the risks they take are worth it.

13.8 billion Years it would take to decode data sent from the Signal.

Signal is an encrypted messaging app. • It is used by hackers, journalists, and government officials. • The biggest risk to Signal security is human error. Someone could be mistakenly added to a chat. Or a device could be lost or stolen.

Think About It Have you ever sent a message to the wrong person? What did you do about it?

The Signal app can be downloaded to a smartphone.

Hacktivists Spy on *Spies*

10

Did you know that some hackers are spies? They snoop on the biggest spies in the world! Hacktivists have attacked the CIA, FBI, and NSA. These federal agencies catch criminals and protect secrets. Hacktivists try to break into their systems. They share hidden information.

One famous group is called "Crackas with Attitude." In 2016, they hacked the CIA and FBI. These agencies should have the strongest security in the world. But one of the hackers didn't think so. They said a 5-year-old could hack the head of the CIA. The group stole private emails and phone numbers of top officials. It published the information. This embarrassed the CIA. The hack exposed serious problems in protection of personal data.

Another famous group is LulzSec. Some of their attacks revealed security weaknesses. One of its members is Hector Xavier Monsegur. He was caught by the FBI.

6,200 Estimated number of **phishing** attacks on federal agencies in 2023. The exact number isn't made public for safety reasons. • These types of attacks are becoming more frequent. • Web-based attacks, like DDoS attacks, are more common as well.

Hackers can be better spies than the top government agencies.

Instead of going to jail, he made a deal. He decided to help the government stop other hackers. He worked with the FBI and helped stop over 300 cyberattacks. Some hacktivists saw him as a traitor. But others respected him. He chose to make the internet safer.

Some people approve of these hacktivists' actions to expose secrets. Others think they are criminals breaking the law. Either way, they are a powerful group. Even the most powerful spies in the world can be hacked!

One hacker thought the CIA's security was so weak, a 5-year-old could hack into it.

LulzSec logo

50 DAYS OF LULZ

50 Days of Lulz was a chaotic time in 2011. Hacktivists in LulzSec launched bold cyberattacks. They targeted big companies, governments, and law enforcement. Their attacks highlighted security flaws in funny ways. Their humor and wit entertained the world. But they also made people think seriously about security.

Governments Create Laws to *Stop Hacktivists*

Governments are working on new rules to address hacktivism. But not everyone agrees on what is right or wrong. For example, there is an R-rated movie called *The Interview*. It is about an American plot to kill the leader of South Korea. North Koreans thought the movie was disrespectful. When it was about to come out in 2015, hacktivists in North Korea reacted. They released private data about the studio and its workers. Their goal was to stop the movie. Many North Koreans supported the hacktivists. But Americans disagreed. They believed the movie was part of their right to free speech.

This event pushed governments to take cyberattacks more seriously. They were especially strong against political hacks. This is when hackers try to change how governments or companies work and do business. More and more countries are passing laws about hacktivism.

Laws don't stop all hackers. They tend to act outside the system anyways. But knowing the boundaries might discourage some hackers. A law outlines when a hack becomes a crime. It makes it easier to charge a hacker.

Countries like China, Russia, and Iran have strict laws against hacktivism. These governments view hacktivists as cybercriminals. They feel laws protect people and important data. Many democratic countries see things a little differently. Hacktivism is largely illegal. But there is more room for debate around what is ethical.

10 Maximum US sentence in years for hackers who steal national security information.

Getting caught a second time can lead to 20 years in jail. • The Computer Fraud and Abuse Act (CFAA) was passed in the United States in 1986. • It is still used to charge hacktivists. • Enforcing laws across international borders relies on goodwill between two nations.

Hacktivists often break laws in order to promote their cause.

A Secret War *Online*

12

A secret war is happening. But it's not with tanks or guns. It's not a battle where people gain or lose territory. It's being fought online. Hackers fight each other every day. Battles are fought with keyboards and computers as weapons. In this world, hacktivists can declare war.

Some people call these fights **cyberterrorism**. It's when hackers try to scare people. They might hurt important computer systems. One famous example is Stuxnet. It was a computer virus. Many experts believe it was used as a weapon. It could slow down a country's nuclear program. It was made to hurt a country without a shot being fired.

Cyberterrorism can look a lot like hacktivism. This can be tricky. Even though hacktivists think they are doing the right thing, they are usually breaking the law. But so do whistleblowers. These leakers share secrets for the good of everyone. And there are laws that can protect them. So, should hacktivists also be protected when they leak secrets? Or should they be punished for their actions? There isn't one answer that everyone agrees on. Doing what is "right" can be complicated. What one person believes is right, another person could see it as wrong.

Hacktivists are not just hackers. They are people who believe in fighting for a cause. Are they heroes? Or are they criminals? Hacktivists remind us that one voice behind a screen can spark a movement.

O The name of a vulnerability in a computer program, called "zero-day."

This is a mistake in a program that nobody knows about yet. • "Zero-day" means that there have been zero days to fix the problem. • It is dangerous because they can be used to steal things or break stuff on computers. • Stuxnet used many zero-day mistakes.

A keyboard can be turned into a weapon if someone has the necessary skills.

Fact

- In December 1998, the hacktivist group Legions of the Underground declared cyber war against Iraq and China. They were protesting of human rights abuses. Their goal was to stop internet access. Other hackers disapproved of this action. They believed the goal opposed the idea of free information access.

- Many hacktivist tools are available to anyone. Tools like Low Orbit Ion Cannon (LOIC), used for DDoS attacks, are often open source. They are easy to use. This can allow even nontechnical users to participate in hacktivism. Little computer knowledge is needed.

Sheet

- Killnet is a pro-Russian hacktivist group. It emerged in 2022. It created DDoS attacks on NATO members. It attacked important infrastructure. The group claims to defend Russia from Western cyber aggression. It shows how hacktivism can support with government interests.

- Jake Davis is known as "Topiary." He was an important spokesperson for LulzSec. He was arrested at age 18 on a remote Scottish island in 2011. His case shows how rural and isolated hacktivists can still reach global influence.

Glossary

activism
Taking action to bring about social or political change.

censorship
The act of blocking or hiding information from the public.

classified
Information that is kept secret by the government.

cybersecurity
Protecting computers and networks from attacks.

cyberterrorism
Using the internet to cause fear or harm.

deface
To damage or ruin the appearance of something.

disrupt
To interrupt or cause problems in a system.

encryption
Turning information into a secret code to keep it safe.

injustice
Unfair treatment or a lack of fairness.

malware
Software that is harmful to computers.

phishing
Tricking people into giving away personal information online.

proxy
A server that acts as a middleman between a user and the internet.

reputation
What people think about someone or something.

terrorist
A person who uses violence to achieve political goals.

VPN
Virtual Private Network; a tool that helps keep your internet activity private.

For More Information

Books

Abdo, Kenny. *Cyber Heists*. Minneapolis: Fly!, an imprint of Abdo Zoom, 2025.

Eason, Sarah. *Hunting a Hacker: Using Science to Crack Cybercrime*. Shropshire, UK: Cheriton Children's Books, 2023.

London, Martha. *Cybersecurity*. Minneapolis: Bearport Publishing Company, 2023.

Olson, Elsie. *Cyber Spying*. Minnesota: Adbo & Daughters, 2025.

Websites

Hackers & Cyber Attacks: Crash Course Computer Science #32
    tpt.pbslearningmedia.org/resource/hackers-cyber-attacks-crash-course-cs/

Meet the Script Kiddies: Teenage Hackers Who Make or Break Our World
    www.youtube.com/watch?v=UaJuXPgn6p8

What Is Hacktivism?
    www.checkpoint.com/cyber-hub/threat-prevention/what-is-hacktivism/

About the Author

Meghan Hatalla is a Minnesota-based writer and UX researcher exploring the intersection of people, technology, and storytelling. She critically examines everything from enterprise AI to historical disasters to create engaging nonfiction for curious minds. When not writing, she's exploring forests, lifting heavy things, or chasing down obscure facts.

Index

activists, 5, 6, 10, 17, 32
Anonymous, 11, 13, 27–28
Arab Spring, 14
attack methods, 8, 12, 17–18, 20, 21, 22, 36, 44

Cablegate, 24, 26
censorship, 14, 16
Crackas with Attitude, 34
cybersecurity, 30

DDoS attacks, 8, 17, 22, 35, 44, 45
defacement, 8
digital movements, 20

eco-hacktivists, 17–18

goals, 8, 10, 11, 12, 14, 21, 27, 28, 37, 44

hacktivist groups, 6, 11, 18, 27, 28, 34, 36, 44, 45
hiding, 27, 30, 32

laws, 5, 36, 37–38, 40, 41
legal consequences, 38
LulzSec, 34, 36, 45

malware, 8
Manning, Chelsea, 24, 26

Occupy Wall Street, 16
Omega, 6
operations, 17, 20, 30

OpSec, 30

phishing, 35
protests, 5, 8, 14, 16, 28, 44

reputations, 11, 22

SeaWorld, 17–18
spying, 34, 36
Stuxnet, 40, 42
suicide hackers, 28

targets, 11, 17, 21, 29, 36
terrorists, 11, 12, 40

WikiLeaks, 9, 10, 26

TOP RANK is published by Black Rabbit Books, P.O. Box 227, Mankato, MN, 56002. • Copyright © 2026 Black Rabbit Books. All rights reserved. No part of this book may be reproduced in any form without written permission from the publisher. • Designed by Danny Nanos • Photographs © Dreamstime/Leo Lintang, 35, Spaceheater, 16, Volodymyr Konko, 15; Getty Images/Darren Staples, 29, Westend61, 2–3, 31; Shutterstock/Ad-Crew, 28, Aspi13, 38, Barry Barnes, 40, 41, Belinda Pretorius, 48, Billion Photos, 20, Brian A Jackson, 44, Casimiro PT, 10, Dmitry Demidovich, 6, g_hang.out, 39, Gorodenkoff, 39, Ixepop, 36, Jolygon, 46–47, Kidsada Manchinda, cover, 1, Klochkov SCS, 27, Lex0077, 45, metamorworks, 9, mipan, cover, 1, Mohammad Bash, 12–13, New Africa, 5, NeydtStock, 8, PhotoVrStudio, 27, Pics6232, 4, Production Perig, 11, Reeh, 2, 42–43, Serhii Yushkov, 37, spatuletail, 5, ssuaphotos, 21, TenPixels, 23, Troyan, 17, vectorfusionart, 42–43, Vereshchagin Dmitry, 22, Visuals6x, 32–33, Vlad G, 18–19, Vladimir Gjorgiev, 25, wk1003mike, 21; Wikimedia Commons/Chelsea Manning, 24, National Park Service, 7, Vin Louisel, 44, Wikileaks, 26; Wikipedia/LulzSec, 36, 45 • Printed in the United States of America.
Library of Congress Cataloging-in-Publication Data is filed under LCCN 2025021468. ISBN 978-1-64582-523-4 (library binding), ISBN 978-1-64582-541-8 (paperback), ISBN 978-1-64582-559-3 (ebook)